A House of Many Windows

Sundress Publications • Knoxville, TN

Editor: Erin Elizabeth Smith
erin@sundresspublications.com
http://www.sundresspublications.com

Colophon: This book is set in Tinos.

Cover Image: Christine Shank, from her *Interiors* series entitled "You Promised to Listen." Find her online at **www.christineshank.com**.

Cover Design: Emily Janowick

Book Design: Erin Elizabeth Smith

A House of Many Windows

Donna Vorreyer

Donna Vorrey
09.18.13

For Sophie –
Sorry to have
missed you at the
reading. Thanks for
thinking of me!
Love,
Mrs. Vorreyer

ACKNOWLEDGEMENTS

Many thanks to the following journals where these poems first appeared, sometimes in earlier versions:

Atticus Review – "What Would It Take to Make a City in Me?"
Autumn Sky Poetry – "After the Storm"
Chantarelle's Notebook – "Misconception"
Exact Change Only – "A Sweet Science"
Literary Mama – "What I Would Show Her", "XXIX," "And My Love Goes With Him"
OVS Magazine – "O'Death"
Rhino Poetry – "Billy Gets the Analogy All Wrong," "Housecleaning Venus"
River Oak Review – "The Leaving Behind"
Sweet: A Literary Confection – "How You Become A Mother"
THIS Literary Magazine – "Other People's Children"
Wicked Alice – "The Black Place," "Many Houses, Many Windows"

"When 'I Don't Love You Anymore' is a Wasp" was made into part of a video triptych by Marc Swoon Bildos and Nic Sebastian: http://vimeo.com/29209281.

The following poems first appeared in the chapbook *Womb/Seed/Fruit* from Finishing Line Press: "Loss Song," "Manhood," "Quick Study," "Now My Teenaged Son Just Tells Me to Go Away," and "Son: In the Blue."

The title line "What Would It Take to Make A City In Me?" is taken from the poem "The Question of my Mother" by Robin Ekiss. In the poem "Domesticity," the phrase "little tell-tale priest" is from the letters of Elizabeth Bishop.

TABLE OF CONTENTS

I. Everything We Think We Need

II. The Weight That It Can Bear

III. Like Lashes, Like Cracks

IV. Something That Sounded Like *Yes*

For Jeff and Dennis, the only home I will ever need.

*The body is a house of many windows: there we
all sit, showing ourselves and crying on the
passers-by to come and love us.*
-Robert Louis Stevenson

I.

Everything We Think We Need

What would it take to make a city in me?

A sturdier frame: steel, iron, infrastructure that will not crack.
Brick, perhaps. Mortar. A mason's sturdy, practiced hand.

Concrete veins with road signs. Bowel Boulevard. Aorta Avenue.
Sparks of firing synapse to light the always-midnight streets.

A good Chinese restaurant in the twists and turns of intestine,
a wide acre of park in the fresh air of expanding lungs.

But a city needs a populace. Children who drool to oil the joints.
Neighbors knocking on the ribcage if the heart beats too loud.

So I prepare to swallow, mouth stretched wide as city sky. I lie
still, hands resting on my belly, wait for the scaffolding to rise.

Anatomy of A Day

I wake in the soft morning of your mouth,
the dawn's horizon in the rise of your hip.
Each body keeps the hours in its own way,
minutes tucked in hollow places,
seconds concealed in a cache of flesh.

The sun travels west, and the heart races
to keep time. Darkness emerges like
a mystery bruise. When your body folds
into mine, glaciers calve. A miracle what
the earth lets go, what our bodies hold.

When *I Love You* is a Meteorite

shooting from the roof of your mouth,
a blazing fireball, ablation melting
and morphing its shape into the surreal.

Sometimes a fall, burning its way out
of the throat with swagger, its long arc
traceable from its first atmospheric breach.

Sometimes a find, black cinder smudge
on the rim of the lips, pulled from under
the tongue in a kiss that singes –
such beautiful immolation.

Upon the Second Attempt, Whole Foods

Care for the container and the fruit will not bruise,
my grandmother would repeat, her own picking basket
smooth and neat, all stray points cut or sanded away.

So we begin to wander, empty-handed, seeking
to maintain the vessel: all organic, free of foreign
substance, feathering a natural nest where a guest

would want to settle, a nest woven to impress
so that any fruit, having spent all summer ripening,
without a blemish to call its own, would wait

for hands to cradle it instead of falling, hard
and half-formed from the branch into the yard.

A Sweet Science

Observe the practiced jab,
the monthly slip, the uppercut –

even gloves cannot prevent
the mask of bruises, eyes barely

visible, lids swelled to walnuts.
Let down the guard. One flow

and the core collapses like
fragile twigs in drought. Still

reeling from the blood, she retreats
to the bathroom, counts to ten,

warms tea in the microwave, ices
her face with frozen peas. Every

scientist is patient. She collects data,
notes patterns. She blows across

the lip of the mug and sips, sweet
honey coating her empty throat.

How to Start Again

Capture the moon, and keep it
tucked in the folds of your robe.

You have hidden more than this: in
small drawers, in boxes, in creases
no iron can flatten. Others have tried
but weakened at its pleading, its
insistence on returning to the sky.

Pay it no mind. You now rule all tides
and cycles, and you have learned
to be hard. Stand at the window like
a woman staring at the sea. Admire
your black handiwork.

Who cares if the night is blind,
its white eye plucked and hooded?
Swathed in fleece against your skin,
the moon births halos at your feet.

After the Third Failure, Silence

She seeks out shadows, pleads guilty,
buys seven different hats to hold the words.

He presses her hands and signs
a litany of sorrows. Still she will not speak.

She wants to give him a gift so simple
that the soil can do it. She cannot.

Crows peck at dropped seeds; the cat
swells with another litter. He goes out

to start the reaping. Generations of fields,
full and ripe with wheat, begin to sing.

Floating Lessons

Curl to nautilus. Remember the blood-rush
wave of the womb and let the water rock you.

Stretch your body across the surface, relax
your muscles, and let your limbs be light. Turn

onto your back, arch to lift your buttocks. Let
your neck fall and submerge your ears. Listen

to the muffled gush of your own breath. Later add
the motion of the arms, the frantic flutter kick. Learn

the sidestroke, the butterfly. Revel in your growing
speed, the churning water in your wake. Nothing will

ever equal the first time you let your body go and
something cradled it, a trust you cannot find again.

When *I Love You* is a Treble Hook

Barbed and caught fast in the most tender tissue,
its silhouette visible on the outside of my cheek.

Metal Cerberus, defying extraction, fingertips pocked
with scars, running with blood. Intrigued, the doctors

shake their heads, stroke the freckled epidermis
of my face with practiced hands. This will not be

pulled easy from the mouth. They prepare to make
a new hole - the only way out, it seems, is through.

.

After the Fourth Failure, Home

You swerve reckless from lane to lane, as if our bodies
were something more than skin, and we grit our teeth
against the distance. In the kitchen, we break bread
seeded with bees. I fill pages with clotted carcasses

of longing, hang them from branches in the yard to
fertilize the tulips we planted last September. We cut
circles of squash, salt the water for the boil, pulverize
our hearts to fine powders we pour down our throats.

Outside the window, the tenderness of fledglings
makes us wish for wings. We press our bodies
against the glass, leave ghost prints with our lips,
mumble lullabies we cannot name to the purple sky.

A House Of Many Windows

open wide to the weather, outside world intruding,
crisp whisper of autumn slipping under its sills,
dullness of summer settling in its sashes

open wide to destruction, hailstorm branches
breaking roof tiles, sliding past jagged stars
of broken casement to crash on the concrete

open for inspection, flung wide in warm spring,
daydreams curtained in linen, every panel clear
unless shades are pulled against the prying light

open wide, a wound, a mouth blowing heated breath
to cloud the pane, to rub a spot clean, murmuring
Here I am. Over here. Let me out.

Instructions for Sleep

Finger the pittance of a mole
on your left hip. Inhale lavender,
both remedy and confection.

Extend one arm overhead and rest
the other beneath the pert plums
of your breasts.

Let your mind become a husk,
its multitude of musts all come
undone.

They will tell you to count sheep.
Do not listen. Conform only
to the moon, its rebel light.

Upon the Fifth Attempt

Every bone
in every wing
of every bird
catches
the current
of my breath.

Every wish a fly
tied to fishing line
arching over a wild
river, a kite in a storm,
trailing a key and
waiting for the strike.

Why I Love You Most When I'm Upset

You are a watched pot,
a willow's easy sway.

You leave only footprints.

You are the exhale,
the rest note, the *shavasana*.

You are lavender and eiderdown.

You are 20/20,
one-twenty over eighty.

I am plutonium.
You are tin.

After the Sixth Failure, IKEA

The dictionary has no word for undoing
expectations, so we go shopping instead.
We buy a headboard, cool and gray as
a gravestone, move onto slick Swedish
clocks, tissue-thin lampshades bordered
with linen, jewel-toned art, any bold or
fragile thing to quell our desire for safety
and pastel. We pile the cart with parts
to build a new fixation, try to fill a hole
in a pail that holds no water. We follow
signs on edges of aisles, prepare our little
wrenches, take everything we think we need.

II.

The Weight That It Should Bear

XXIX

Twenty-nine is the tenth prime number,
a Lucas prime, a Pell prime, a tetrannacci.

A Pillai prime, an Eisenstein prime with no
imaginary part, the sixth Sophie Germain.

A Markov number, a Perrin number, aliquot
sum of odd discrete primes. Atomic number

of copper. Approximate days in a lunar month.
Number of years for Saturn to orbit the sun.

Alphabets letters in Turkish, Finnish, Faroese,
Danish, Swedish and Norwegian. Highest

possible score in cribbage. Highest possible
hand in Khanhoo. The number of *suras*

in the Qur'an that begin with *muqatta'et*.
The age my womb was declared *condemned*.

Misconception

For two years, I watched news stories about teens
abandoning newborns in dumpsters, fifty-something

grandmothers serving as surrogates, third world
women wandering dirty streets with five six seven

children hanging on their thin arms, all of them
successful. I think I knew even before the blood

before needles injected me with dye so I could
watch it shoot through my Fallopian tubes

like some twisted neon sign. Here in this sterile office
filled with plastic fetuses nestled in cutaway models

of flesh, I accept my failure as a female, my uterus
some abandoned cubicle. A lesser man could not

love something broken, but mine sits next to me,
knowing there is no blame, all his lovely sperm

condemned to swim forever in ardent circles,
lost children floundering, finding nowhere to root.

Housecleaning Venus

after "Venus de Milo with Drawers"
by Salvador Dali, Art Institute of Chicago

Pluck the mink tufts of her nipples
to peek inside her breasts – remove
the fear of lumps, the spoiled milk.

Pull the slim drawer beneath her ribs-
sort the swirling mass of secrets, words
swallowed and stuck, her burning lungs.

Attack her navel next – dump its musty
contents out, useless skin, hollowed
pockets, rumblings of endless hunger.

Unpack the vertical beneath her knee-
shin splints and frail fragments of bone,
the deflated balloons of old bruises.

Save the forehead drawer for last. Explore
mazes full of mirrors, memories of arms
that remain muscled, smooth and whole.

What to Do When There is No Ark

Once, in a dream, I was drowning
on the street, trapped inside a car.
I did not pray, but escaped by window,

swam to safety clutching a porch rail,
the oaks arching into buttresses, sky
stained dark and purple as Lenten glass.

When I awoke, it was pouring, stray
cats scratching at the screen door,
turning the soft nothing of night

into ceremony, something like a cathedral –
a stone, a star, a sign – miraculous and
impossible as the rounding of this broken

womb. Across the road, rain pools along
the curb, swelling that wants to be a flood.
Inside I busy myself with dams.

Another Truth the Dead Know

Gone, like the dinosaurs are gone, buried in tar or dust, reduced to fossilized puzzles, jumbled lonely bones. Now it is finally June – sun and flowers in full swing can't bring you back. I drink from glasses brimming with ice, eat pink steaks from the grill, embrace these pleasures of the body in lieu of your touch. It is what I have built, a temple of things I can control.

My nights stretch endless on the edge of sleep, dreams like water against my skull. We are both there, but not alone. The dinosaurs chase us with their snarling teeth and tiny arms. We are trapped at the edge of a lake, and boats arrive just in time to spirit us away. I am trying to hang on, concrete scraping away the knucklebone. All I can do is sleep again and bleed. And bleed.

The Black Place

after the painting by Georgia O'Keefe

is dull
is gray
is sallow
is skin
is blurry
is dimpled
is dough
is not

is beige
is round
is soft
is crevice
is safe
is rising
is landscape
is not

is smooth
is blurred
is eggshell
is sandy
is thigh
is secret
is whisper
is not

is smoke
is folding
is surface
is hip
is buttock
is light
is secret
is not black

The Ghosts of Summer Mothers

whisper polite behind privet hedges
tuck in your tags and smooth your edges

smell of sunscreen, tomatoes on the vine
steal the biggest pickle from the brine

gawk at the neighbor's garish gnomes
tsk over your shoulder while you write poems

circle like planets stacked with halos
hover in a charcoal hibachi haze of smoke

praise the moxie of the asphalt double-dutch
reach out transparent hands that cannot touch

Other People's Children

Narrow their velvet-painting eyes
at the mention of *no*. Kick the back
of your seat on transatlantic flights.
Spit crickets in the quiet of a theater.

Know how to reset your password.
Carry the old world in cupped hands.
Gather around to gawk at it, this ugly
curious insect they only want to smash.

When *I Don't Love You Anymore* is a Wasp

Parasitic, predatory, she flaps two sets of wings
against my tongue, builds a papery nest that absorbs

my saliva, sucks my mouth dry. I stutter out nonsense
to avoid the prick of her ovipositor, its paralytic venom.

It would be easy to avoid this. It would be easy to gag her
out, separate her thorax with my teeth, silence her buzz,

but she is insistent. She wants me to spit her with wild
velocity, stinger first, straight into your patient face.

After the Storm

As if they knew,
the clouds float
back-and-forth,
scribbled, as if you
had tried to erase
the sky, as if you
held some grudge
against the weather
or the atmosphere
or a certain shade
of blue, as if you
could command
the horizon, as if
the words spoken
could be taken back,
as if you could erase
anything at all, as
if the past was not
indelible, as if.

Extermination

My lungs burn, sharp
with juniper, pine,
impending ice.

Ahead, the trail slants
into the white-capped
hills, too far today

for my tired boots. I turn
toward my house instead,
put the silver kettle on

the fire, warm the palms
of my hands. The storm
swells then bursts, spills

small, scattered flakes
that gather and shimmer
on the sill like scales

of Arctic fish. The trails
disappear, whitewash
sprinkled with stains

of bark or branch not yet
buried. Sequins of sugar
dissolve in my tea.

I have scraped a simple
winter far from where
I want to be. Wrapped

in blankets, I read your
yellowed letters, wait
for them to sing to me

the way they sang before,
when nothing could kill
us. Silverfish flicker

across the pages. I crush
and smear one, its metallic
slick blurring your name.

Outside the snow falls.
Inside, a sudden desire
for the stinging kiss of salt.

After the Fight, In the Kitchen

A bastard apple tumbles
outside the rim of the fruit
bowl, orbiting the obedient
oranges and pears like some
angry red planet. Both you

and breakfast storm in wearing
plastic jackets. The roof counts
each raindrop and one finite ray
of sun resigns to be lonely as
the door sticks against its stop.

Bile is called back into the throat.
I pull smoked fish from its bones.
You slice bagels, and pain exits above
the slash. Something divine escapes,
breaking our silence and our fast.

III.

Like Lashes, Like Cracks

Cleft

Art is our chief means of breaking bread with the dead.
                    -W.H. Auden

This morning is a symphony of breaking,
percussion rim shots in my bones.
Outside, wind bends branches into domes.

Not one thing remains whole: not the eggs
cracked into a chipped bowl, not the car,
nicked with wear, not even my sleep.

Seething beneath all my surfaces, something
prepares to burst seams, brews deep. Fragments
rule my universe – the terse words of my spouse,

of grocery clerks – and, being accustomed
to parts, I become a master of gaps, the art
of putting things back together, clamps

to hold pieces, planes to shave edges
into joints. Time wedges rifts into valleys.
The apple can't escape the worm inside it,

slow tunneling decay. I struggle to close
the door, bulging like yeast in the daily bread
I pound and braid and break with the dead.

Still Tending Each Garden

My tiny truth, my traveler. Forgive
those who insist you are gone.

They do not know the swell and heft
of you still seeded in my memory,
my slip, my shoot, my fruitless bud.

My grace note, my disembodied echo,
your hum rumbles through my limbs,
a melody unfinished, without a refrain.

Some days, I hear you, calling from
an unseen place in umbilical code,
my confidante, my secret semaphore.

My uncoupled sonnet, my comma
splice. Forgive the mediocre world,
ill-versed in our intimate literacy.

I know our story continues, my sweet
ellipsis, my unresolved ampersand.

O' Death

I am tired of living in your slate house,
this neighborhood with the red cottage
on one side, silver mansion on the other.

You used to have that bad boy swagger,
shrouded in black and wielding a blade,
your gaunt grin a secret to decode.

You offered certainty, so I never missed
the world's risks and miseries. Now I am
through with the constancy. Give me orange

juice spilled on a white table, blood-red tissue
blooms after shaving. I know what I want
and it isn't you. I want the misstep, the breaking.

The One Where I Remember Flight

Two cardinals beat a laser beam from my roof
to the backyard pine as I choke on my own thick
phlegm and my bones click in gunshot rhythm.

The weatherman says no rain but the sky
is heavy-lidded and gray and the red birds skitter
from perch to perch, warbling. I am stranger now,

some hardened resin grounding awkward feet,
and red birds who used to eat from my hand shoot
their flaming bodies like arrows a distance away.

Once I was a bird, my bones light, my feathers
fluffed and ignited with air, but each spine molted
and left me with this clumsy weight of flesh,

so hard to carry. I once held fortune in my beak –
a piece of straw, a worm – and had no worries except
a hint of rain, a furtive cat, and the wind, the wind.

Loss Song

Winter Sunday, furnace groaning overtures
all out of tune. Crust of sleep shakes from
your eyes like sugar, like salt, like the plinking

of pizzicato strings. Listen for the maraca
skittering of beetles, the pianissimo glissando
of wind and rain. Float curls of your shorn

hair in the sink, open and close the scissors
against the dark, thin cymbals that swish
with friction and forgetting. The road bends

like

jazz, like the crooked wah-wah of a trumpet.
Plug a mute into that horn. Play it again.

What the Twilight Says

A circle of starlings rises in formation,
a rush of wings. Something stirs in my chest,
a stutter of longing that wants to be a blaze.

Night takes credit for stars, and day makes
the hours tremble and shine. I drop hints to
lovers on idle walks and night shift workers

as they shuffle into factories. Say I build bridges
between extremes, pull a thread, ignite desires,
revolve doors. I am the book you have not read,

the film that freezes in the reel, slow burning
a hole into the still frames of day. I am the grocer
who knows you are starving and cannot pay.

I am dust trapped in the grooves of an old LP,
skipping *please don't go,* the yawns of a thousand
lost days growling in the back of your throat.

Domesticity

I throw open the curtains and clap sofa cushions. Puffs
of blue dust swirl. I spend the day uncovering surprises.

Your hammer in the bathroom. Your hat crammed in the drawer.

I catch my face in the mirror, lips colorless, sucked dandelion
stems. I do not clean the glass, little tattle-tale priest, showing all.

Branches brush the windows, remind me of a mountain town.

Here at the shore, flying fish leave long scratches across
the surface of the waves. I reach out to clear away the marks.

Lament

Don't be fooled by autumn, each scarlet leaf
a ruse of death, a pretty fallacy -
we all know that branch will bud again. Grief
is a temporary thing for a tree,
lacks the weight that it should bear, the richness
of its taste, the sting of vinegar
on the tongue. Real grief settles in, nests
between the lungs and the ribcage, each word
a loathsome chore. Nature lacks conviction,
changes its fickle moods at whim, rains Bach
then thunders Wagner, bends its cruel diction
to soft moss and unshakable rock
and then forgets, begins each day anew.
Grief requires memory. I remember you.

The Turning

Flowers in the back garden die,
their withered petals parchment
ghosts of their summer selves.

I have no quarrel with death. It sways
in the breeze like laundry, leans
at the threshold each morning as I rise

for work. It is not the frightening Death
of childhood, no black-robed menace
of Dickens, Poe. Just a woman

at her window, face tender as the bark
of spring birch, white, unblemished.
I almost forget about death on days

like this, the autumn sky broken only
by branches, black, like lashes, like
cracks on the lapis-glazed eye of God.

IV.

Something That Sounded Like *Yes*

Billy Gets the Analogy All Wrong

a woman without children, a gate through which no
one had entered the world.
        -Billy Collins

As if a woman were a gate –

    an arena door guarded
    by a muscle-bound bouncer
    and velvet rope, children
    waving twenties and straining
    to catch their names on the list

    or ornate wrought-iron
    shut tight with chains
    and padlocks, babies
    banging at the bars, bruising
    their tender, tiny fists.

Let me tell you what a woman is –

    not the gate but the sentry,
    ushering the lost to refuge,

    not the entrance, but the stage,
    action all unfolding from her wings,

    not the shuttered womb,
    but the unlatched heart, wide open.

How You Become A Mother

You are a little ashamed that one of your first thoughts is *I could have been a slut in high school*, all of those boys who wanted to touch you, fear of pregnancy trumping every primal urge, and you wonder what it would have been like. You sit and listen to your pregnant friends bemoan their swollen feet, their five-minute bladders. They confer about vitamins, breathing techniques. They worry about doctors and vaccines and which breast pump to buy. You listen politely, have nothing to add. They ask if they should change the subject. You say no. You sit in the social worker's office, and she asks you what sort of child you would like to adopt. The only answer you can think of is *human*. You have to write about your whole life, the therapist's foot tapping in time with her pen as she grills you about your parents, your childhood, your definition of *family*. You have to circle *yes* or *no* on checklists: would you adopt a child without a limb? With a heart condition? You are a monster whenever you circle *no*. You stare at a picture over and over. This will be your son. You send off your fingerprints, are rubber-stamped by two different countries. You wait for everything to be ready. You stare at a picture. This will be your son. You are delayed by the state's red tape, so you enlist the help of your senator, your congressman. Two months later, you are cleared. You stare at a picture. This will be your son. You can wait to travel, or the escort overseas can bring him now. You say *get on the plane*. Now your friends have had the babies, and you listen to horror stories about stitches, jaundice, and incubators. They complain about stretch marks, tender breasts, delirium from lack of sleep. They blend their own organic carrot mush, obsess over breastfeeding benefits and percentiles for length and weight. They ask for your opinion. You can only remember how you waited at the airport, how you held your breath as you lifted him from the stroller and your whole body just knew what to do.

What I Would Show Her

He is a shark under the blankets,
some part of him continually in
motion yet never waking. I like
the way his forehead sweats, even
in the cold Chicago winter, fine
black hair decoupaged to his skin,
bronze skin that flakes with a filmy
layer of white in dry weather.

He sighs and smacks his lips, exhales
loose teeth and peppermint. I should
tell you how much I like his ears, fuzzy
shells where I listen for the sea
of his pulse, round like my ears, a feature
we share despite no common DNA.
His lashes fan out like peacock feathers
on his cheek after hiding all day

in the folds of his eyes. Let's talk about
his arms. His pudgy wrists have folds, his
hands seemingly screwed on like an old
G.I. Joe, his palms sweaty. I love holding
his feet, fragile and warm as hairless puppies
in my hands, each toe a pink pearl I could
rub against my teeth to assure it's real.

I could go on - his belly a firm melon,
his eyebrows black commas, his white
teeth snow volcanoes erupting from his
gums — but it's such a cliché for a mother
to watch her child in sleep. I apologize. I can't
help myself. I do it because I never thought
I would. I do it for her because she never will.

Quick Study

At six, he already knows
how to wound. *My real mom
would be nicer.* He knows

the words cut, but not how
deep, how they sucker punch,
leave me breathless, real blood

rushing through my real veins,
real stone of worry nestled in
my mother's heart. He knows,

so he tosses them like candy
wrappers, sows them like seeds,
stomps them off his shoes like

snow. Undaunted, I pick them
up, pull them out by the roots,
wipe away the footprints

and guide his steps toward me
who kisses his real forehead,
wipes his real tears every night.

The Wound

It does not even look like skin, the flesh
peeled away in curls, gray but tinted
with blood, flecked with gravel and dirt.

The center is deep, a hole where a hole
should not be. I irrigate, apply pressure,
pour the bubbling peroxide dead center

and hold his leg still as he flinches, this
son who has asked for my assistance,
a rare thing, this asking.

A mother prefers a wound that she can
see. More frightening are the hidden ones
that fester in hot tears, in anger, in long

silences punctuated by the slamming
of doors. The peroxide sizzles, a sign
that it is working. If only I could see

the healing of those secret places, the mad
gash of living that widens each day, then
scabs only to break, to leave its scars.

Now My Teenaged Son Just Tells Me to Go Away

I remember the moon
of his face rising over
the table top, crescent
slip of smile content
and curious, tiny flakes
of dry skin dotting his
velvet head like stars.

I love you to the moon,
he used to say, rest his
golden cheek against
my knee in the slant
of evening, his caress
filled to bursting with
supernovas, sweet kisses.

He is a constant source,
still the first light I seek,
both dim and beaming,
master of phases. I should
have known. Somewhere
inside him, a man's face
was always looming.

Son: In the Blue

When a snake is preparing to shed its skin, it is said to be "in the blue." The skin becomes dull, the eyes become cloudy, and there is an increase in nervous behavior due to the fact that it cannot see well.

I find old skins
at the bottom
of your hamper,
stuffed under
your unmade bed,
ghost copies
of your pattern
and shape pulsed
off in one piece.

You cannot bear
to be touched, this
new self, raw
and untested as
you emerge. Afraid
to handle you in this
state, I adopt a love
of distance. But

a mother is nothing
if not a shield. Shed
the caps from your
eyes. I am coiled
at your feet, poised
to sink my fangs
into a world that wants
to keep you nervous,
dull, and blinded.

Manhood

I hear it rattling in the slow burn
of his bundled slumber, the chirp
of his child's voice dipped to deep
bass even in murmuring sleep.

Exertion brushes him with a musky
sheen, more stench than sweetness
in his sweat, the smooth skin of
his upper lip seeded with dark weeds.

I cannot lift the ladder he carries across
the yard, the soft body I cradled now
hardened to muscle. I cannot keep him
from all the mistakes a man will make.

The Leaving Behind

My son greets me on my forty-fifth birthday with
the observation that I am now halfway to dead, as if
that is a destination, a stop at a dingy railroad station

where the middle-aged are forced off with their bags
before the conductor waves and the engine lurches
toward some central hub of innocence, of arrogance,

some *we-never-close*, shining-bright city of youth.
He does not know that I have stopped before, each stage
of the journey marked by where I paused and scanned

the landscape. Consider the undulating snake of time,
the infinite arrivals, departures, each a casting off of dead
skin. See my husk on the platform. I am still traveling.

And My Love Goes With Him

in bursts of static song over a short-wave radio
in the coldest winter tucked into his blue wool socks

through the red, muddy water in the gutter after rain
in the cornerstone of the ground floor of his dormitory

woven into the wonderful purple of a southern twilight
and the strutting peacock of a clear mid-afternoon sky

up a steep ladder, down a steep hill: wherever he draws
breath: the oxygen, the carbon, the nitrogen, the pine

Many Houses, Many Windows

Not my house. Not my windows. Not my sorry
story, my bitter cherries. Not my laundry, my orange
peels, my backpack. I should have said not *just* my house.

Many houses, many windows. Many stories, many fruits
(pitted and peeled), many bags and pillowcases. I observe
many houses and live in one. I polish my windows and look

through others. I do not know why I mentioned fruit.
I do not eat cherries or oranges, but it sounded like the sort
of thing that many would understand. My linens get dirty;

I have a need to carry things. But it is not *just* my house.
Think of the doors you have walked through and thought
I'm home. The windows you have opened near your bed

on a hot night. The lives you would have led
had one of them been nailed or painted shut.

When You Ask Me If I Am Happy

I cannot tell the truth – I swear
it is not in my machinery,

something damaged in
production, a little mix-up

of wires and switches,
neurons that osculate but

do not spark. Stop. Do not ask
me again. This morning, the sky

burned so blue, my bones
ached to touch it, and you grazed

the back of my neck to shiver.
Something rose in my throat,

something ancient and erupting,
something that sounded like *yes.*

ABOUT THE POET

Donna Vorreyer is the author of four chapbooks: *The Imagined Life of the Pioneer Wife* (Redbird Chapbooks), *Womb/Seed/Fruit* (Finishing Line Press), *Come Out, Virginia* (Naked Mannekin Press), and *Ordering the Hours* (Maverick Duck Press). She is a poetry editor for *Mixed Fruit*, and her work has appeared in many journals, recently in *Sweet, Linebreak, Rhino, Cider Press Review, Stirring,* and *Wicked Alice*. Donna lives in the Chicago area where she teaches middle school and therefore often acts like she is twelve years old.

SUNDRESS PUBLICATIONS TITLES

Gathered: Contemporary Quaker Poets
Ed. by Nick McRae
$16.00 ISBN 978-1-939675-01-9

The Hardship Post
Jehanne Dubrow
$14.00 ISBN 978-1-939675-03-3

Too Animal, Not Enough Machine
Christine Jessica Margaret Reilly
$10.00 ISBN 978-1-939675-02-6

The Old Cities
Marcel Brouwers
$14.00 ISBN 0-9723224-9-3

One Perfect Bird
Letitia Trent
$14.95 ISBN 0-9723224-8-5

Like a Fish
Daniel Crocker
$14.95 ISBN 0-9723224-8-5

The Bone Folders
T.A. Noonan
$14.95 ISBN 0-9723224-6-9

Especially the Deer
Tyurina Allen, Mary Beth Magin,
& Julie Ruble
$12.95 ISBN 0-9723224-0-X

CPSIA information can be obtained at www.ICGtesting.com
Printed in the USA
LVOW06s1935060913

351360LV00003B/14/P